My First  n

Most Reverend Louis LaRavoire
Former Bishop of Krishnagar, India

"As the Father loves me, so I also love you.
Remain in my love." (John 15:9)

OUR MISSION HOUSE
Sisters of Mary Immaculate
118 Park Road
Leechburg, PA 15656

About the Book

Bishop Morrow published his book, My First Communion, in English for the first time in 1936 in Manila, Philippines. Later it was published also in seven dialects of the Philippines. More editions followed in Spanish, Japanese, Italian, English (U.S.), and several Indian languages.

Over the years more than 12,000,000 copies were published.

Revised Edition – 2010

Illustrations by Joseph W. Little

Visit our website: www.omhsmi.org

Printed in the United States of America

CONTENTS

A Word to Parents, Catechists and Teachers

Holy Mass is the greatest and most pleasing act of worship that can be offered to God. Holy Communion is an integral part of the Holy Mass. When a child receives the first Holy Communion, it is the first time the child offers the Mass in a complete manner.

My First Holy Communion was prepared for children, although it can help adults as well. The book contains all that a child needs to know before receiving first Holy Communion. It attempts to teach the loveliness and the truth of the teachings of our Lord Jesus Christ, our Savior and Friend.

More than any other person will a child do anything for love. This book aims at helping children develop a great personal love for God, so that they will not only learn their religion more easily, but will also live it more faithfully.

+Bishop Morrow

God and Everything

In the beginning God was all alone.

There was no one else, only God.

There was nothing at all.

Then God made all things.

God made the day. He made the sky.

He made the land and the sea.

He made the sun, the moon, the stars.

God made plants, birds, fishes, and

other animals. He made everything.

God made all these things out of nothing.

He made everything out of nothing.

God only said, "Let there be".

And lo! Everything was made!

Out of nothing there came light!

The world was made!!

The sun and moon and stars all were created.

It was long, long ago that God did this wonderful work.

Who was all alone in the beginning? When did God make all things? What were some of the things God made? What did God use to make all these things? Can any one else make everything out of nothing? How did God make everything?

Did God make all things?

Yes, God made all things.

God was always God forever and forever.
God always lived. He had no beginning.
God will always live. He will not stop living.
He will never have an end. God will never die.
God always was, and he always will be.
We cannot see God, because he is a spirit.
A spirit does not have a body like ours.
We cannot see a spirit.

But God is here just the same. He is in all places.
God is in heaven and on earth. He is in our hearts.
He is everywhere.

God is my most loving and tender Father.
He loves me and wants me to go to heaven.

God is so wonderful that he does not need anything to
make him better.
This is why we say God is perfect. No one is perfect
except God.

When did God become God?
When did God begin to live?
Will God ever stop living?
Where is God?
Why do we say God is perfect?
Who besides God is perfect?

Did God have a beginning?
No, God had no beginning; he always was.

Will God always be?
Yes, God will always be.

Where is God?
God is everywhere.

Is God good?
**Yes, God is very good and most wonderful.
He is a loving Father to all.**

What God Can Do

God made the world and everything else.

He can do anything and everything.

Nothing that God does is hard for him to do.

It was not hard for him to make heaven and earth.

God knows all things. He knows what happened from the very beginning.

He knows what will happen in all the years to come.

God knows what we think. He knows what we say.

He knows what we do.

God sees us and everything we do.

He hears us and everything we say.

He knows when we are bad and when we are good.

God knows all things. We can never hide anything from him.

If I take a ball and hide in the ground, God will see me.

He will see the ball hidden in the ground.

God can see us, whatever we do, or wherever we are. We
cannot hide from God.

What can God do? Was it hard for God to make everything
out of nothing?
What does God know? Does he know what happened many,
many years ago?
Does he know what will happen many, many years from now?
What does God know about us? Can we do anything that God
does not see? Can we hide anything from God?

Can God do all things?
Yes, God can do all things.

Does God know all things?
Yes, God knows all things.

God made all things.

God made the angels, very, very good. He wanted them to live with him always.

But some angels became very bad. They did not want to do what God wanted. They disobeyed God. That was very wrong.

It is a sin not to obey God. Doing wrong is sin. Disobeying God is sin.

Disobedience to God's laws is sin.

The bad angels committed a serious sin and made God sad. That was the first sin ever committed. Sin makes God sad.

God punished the bad angels for their sin. The bad angels became devils.

God took the good angels to heaven. Heaven is the home of God. The angels will live with God forever and forever.

God punished the devils in hell. They are there now in hell. They will suffer there forever and forever.

Who made angels? Did God make the angels good or bad? How did some angels become bad? Did the bad angels do right or wrong? What is disobeying God called? Does God like sin? What did the bad angels become? What did God do for the good angels?   What is heaven? What did God do to the bad angels? How long will the angels stay in heaven with God? How long will the devils stay in hell?

What is sin?
Sin is disobedience to God's laws.

Who committed the first sin?
The bad angels committed the first sin.
They were disobedient to God.

Adam and Eve

Long, long ago, God made all things.

Last of all, God made human beings in his own
image and likeness. God made the first man and
named him Adam. God also made the first woman.
Her name was Eve.

Adam and Eve were the first people on earth.
All the people of the world are children of Adam and
Eve. We have all come from the first man and the
first woman.
That is why we call Adam and Eve our first parents.
Adam was the father and Eve the mother of all
humankind ever born, of everybody.
God loved our first parents very much. He made
them very good.
God gave Adam and Eve a beautiful garden for their
home.
This garden where Adam and Eve lived was called
paradise.

Who was the first man? Who was the first woman?
Who were the first people on earth? Why do we call
Adam and Eve our first parents? What did God do
for Adam and Eve? Where did our first parents live?

Who were the first man and woman?
**The first man and woman were
Adam and Eve.**

God made me, he is my Father. I am his child. God loves me. He wants me to go to heaven some day and be happy with him always. He is happy when I am good. He is sad when I am bad.

God takes care of me all the time. He gave me my parents, brothers, and sisters and friends.

God gave me an angel for my very own. This good angel is my Guardian Angel.

God is good. He wants to make me happy with him in heaven some day. That is why God made me.

God sees all I do. He sees me at home, at school, at play. He sees me when I sleep.

God hears all I say. I must not say bad words because God will hear and be sad.

God does everything for me. What can I do to be happy with him? I can pray to him, work for him, play for him. I must know him, love him, serve him. I must do everything for him.

I will be good because I want to be happy with God in heaven some day. God loves me. I love God.

Who made you? Where does God want you to go?
What has God done for you? What does God know
about you? What can you do to be happy with God?

Who made you?
God made me.

Why did God make you?
**God made me to show his goodness and to
make me happy with him in heaven.**

*What must you do to be happy with God
in heaven?*
**To be happy with God in heaven I must know
him, love him, and serve him in this world
and help others to do so.**

7   My Guardian Angel

God gave me my Guardian Angel to watch over me. I cannot see my Angel because angels have no body like mine. My Guardian Angel is a spirit.

My Guardian Angel is with me day and night, and loves me. My Guardian Angel wants me always to be a good child of my heavenly Father. My Angel is with me when I play, when I study, when I sleep and sees me all the time.

My Guardian Angel watches over me, helps me and protects me from the evil one. He is sad when I am naughty. If I feel like being bad, I will pray to my Guardian Angel, who will help me.

I will say to my Angel often:

> ***ANGEL OF GOD**, my guardian dear,*
> *to whom his love commits me here,*
> *ever this day (or night) be at my side,*
> *to light and guard, to rule and guide. Amen.*

This is the same as saying: "Dear Guardian Angel, God gave you to me because he loves me. Help me always. Do not let me hurt God at all."

Why did God give you a Guardian Angel? Why can you not see your Angel? When is your Angel with you? When does your Angel see you? Is your Guardian Angel happy when you are naughty? What will you say to your Guardian Angel when you feel like being bad? Say the "Angel of God".

What does your Guardian Angel do for you?
My Guardian Angel watches over me, helps me and protects me from the evil one.

8   The Sin of Adam and Eve

God put Adam and Eve in Paradise. He wanted them to go to heaven after a little while. He wanted them to be happy with him forever.

Adam and Eve were very happy in Paradise. Everything they wanted was there.

They could have everything except the fruit of one tree. God told them to take everything except that fruit.

But one day the devil came in the form of a snake. He told Eve to eat of the fruit. And she did. She also made Adam eat of it.

Our first parents did not obey God. They did wrong. They committed sin. Disobeying God is sin. Disobedience to God's laws is sin.

Adam and Eve listened to the devil and not to God. They disobeyed God and committed sin.

Because of their sin, they lost God's love and intimate friendship. And their sin is passed on to all of us. It comes to us from the origin of humankind.

Adam and Eve were our first parents. Their sin in us is called the original sin.

What could Adam and Eve have in Paradise ? What could they not have? What did God tell them not to take?

Who committed the first sin on earth ?
Our first parents, Adam and Eve, committed the first sin on earth.

9   The Punishment of Adam and Eve

God sees everything. He saw the sin of Adam and Eve.
He was very sad and angry.

God hates sin. He hated the sin of Adam and Eve. He
punished them. He sent them out of Paradise, and closed
heaven to them.

Adam and Eve could not go to heaven because they lost
God's love and friendship by their sin. All the people to be
born afterwards could not go to heaven because of the sin
of their first parents, Adam and Eve.

All of us lost heaven because of the sin of Adam and Eve.
Their loss passed on to all of us, their children.

If wealthy parents lose all their wealth, it affects their
children. In the same way, our first parents' loss of God's
love and friendship affected us too, because Adam and
Eve were our first father and mother. The sin of Adam
and Eve in us is called the original sin. We are all born
with original sin.

What did God think of the sin of Adam and Eve? What
did God do to Adam and Eve? Why could not Adam and
Eve go to heaven? Why could not their children go to
heaven? How do we suffer on account of their sin?
What sin do all of us have when we are born? What is the
sin of Adam and Eve in us called?

Is this sin passed on to us from Adam and Eve?
**Yes, this sin is passed on to us from Adam
and Eve.**

What is this sin in us called?
This sin in us is called original sin.

10   Three Persons in One God

God is three persons. I am only one person.
The three persons in God are the Father, the Son, and the
Holy Spirit. God is not one person only.
God the Father is the first person.
God the Son is the second person.
God the Holy Spirit is the third person.

Each person is God. The Father is God. The Son is God.
The Holy Spirit is God.

Each person is God. But all three persons are only one God.
We call the three persons in one God the Blessed Trinity.

I believe that there are three persons in one God because
God said so. I have God's word for it.

God cannot tell a lie. The Blessed Trinity is three persons in
one God.

Is there only one God?
Yes, there is only one God.

How many persons are there in God?
**In God there are three persons the Father, the
Son, and the Holy Spirit.**

What do we call the three persons in one God?
We call the three persons in one God the Blessed Trinity.

How do we know that there are three persons in one God?
We know that there are three persons in one God because we have God's word for it.

The Sign of the Cross

There are three persons in one God.

I show that I believe this when I make the Sign of the Cross.

I say, **"In the name of the Father, and of the Son, and of the Holy Spirit. Amen."**

God the Son is the second person. He came down on earth.

He became a man because he loved us.

God the Son died on the cross because he loved us . God the Son is Jesus.

I show that I believe this when I make the Sign of the Cross well. It makes me think of God the Son dying on the cross.

When I make the Sign of the Cross, I make God happy.

When I say, "In the name of," he knows I mean to say,

"Dear God, I want to do this all for you."

Before I sleep, when I awake, before I eat, before I study, I shall make the Sign of the Cross.

I shall ask a blessing for myself, saying slowly:
"In the name of the Father, and of the Son, and of the Holy Spirit. Amen."

What did God the Son do for us? How did he die?
What was the name of God the Son? What two things
do you show when you make the Sign of the Cross?
What do you mean when you say, "in the name of"?
When do you make the Sign of the Cross?

Make the Sign of the Cross

27

All the people of the world lost heaven because of the sin of Adam and Eve, our first parents.

God was very sorry for all the people of the world. He wanted them to go to heaven and be with him. So he sent down his Son to help them.

The Son of God is Jesus Christ. Jesus is the second person made man. Jesus is true God.

God the Son became man to help everybody to go to heaven. Jesus Christ is true man.

Jesus Christ is true God and true man.

God sent an angel to a pure and holy virgin. The virgin's name was Mary. The angel told Mary that God wanted her to be the Mother of Jesus.

The angel said, "Hail, full of grace, the Lord is with thee. Blessed art thou among women."

This is the same as saying, "Be happy! You are pleasing to God! He loves you and blesses you more than all other women!"

God chose the Virgin Mary to be the Mother of Jesus. This is why the angel called her blessed.

The words of the angel are in the "Hail Mary". I pray like the angel when I say the "Hail Mary."

What did God do to help the people of the world?

Did one of the persons of the Blessed Trinity become man?
Yes, the second person, the Son of God, became man.

What is the name of the Son of God made man?
The name of the Son of God made man is Jesus Christ.

Is Jesus Christ both God and man?
Yes, Jesus Christ is both God and man.

The Blessed Virgin Mary went to see her cousin Saint Elizabeth. When Saint Elizabeth saw Mary, she said, "Blessed is the fruit of thy womb."
It was like saying, "Blessed is your Child."
These beautiful words are in the "Hail Mary," that I say every day. Mary's Child is blessed, because he is God.
Jesus was born on Christmas Day. Christmas is the birthday of Jesus. He was born in Bethlehem.

Jesus was born in a stable. He was born poor because he loves the poor. He wanted to be poor.
Angels sang sweetly in the sky. They told some shepherds to go and see the baby Jesus. The shepherds went and found Jesus with Mary and Joseph. How happy they were! Kneeling, they adored Jesus.

Three kings from the East came to see Jesus. A star showed them the way. They brought the Child Jesus gifts of gold, frankincense and myrrh. Kneeling, they adored Jesus.

I will also adore Jesus. He became a poor child for love of me. I will love all the poor. I will share what I have with others.

 Who was Saint Elizabeth? What did she say to the
Blessed Virgin Mary? Where can we find those words?
What is Christmas? Where was Jesus born ? Who is his
Mother? Who told the shepherds to see the Child Jesus?
Who came from the East to see Jesus? What gifts did
they bring to the Child Jesus?

When was Jesus born?
**Jesus was born on the first Christmas Day,
more than two thousand years ago.**
Who is the Mother of Jesus?
**The Mother of Jesus is the Blessed
Virgin Mary.**

The Blessed Virgin Mary is the Mother of Jesus. She is the Mother of God because Jesus is God.
The Blessed Virgin Mary is also my Mother. Jesus gave her to me before he died.

I love the Blessed Virgin Mary very much. She is our Blessed Mother. She is our beloved Mother.

God loved our Blessed Mother very much. He made her soul all beautiful and good. She was happy to do everything that God wished her to do.

Our Blessed Mother was the only person created without original sin. She was always holy. This is why we call her "Holy Mary."
The Blessed Mother loves me. I am her child. I want to be like her and please our Father in heaven.
I pray, "My Mother, help me to be good like you. I want to love the poor because you and Jesus love them."

Who is the Blessed Virgin Mary? Is she the Mother of God? Did our Blessed Mother have original sin like us? Who was the only person God made all beautiful and good?

Was any one ever free from original sin?
Yes, the Blessed Virgin Mary was free from
original sin.

Say the "Hail Mary."

Hail Mary, full of grace,
     the Lord is with thee.
     Blessed are thou among women,
     and blessed is the fruit of thy womb, Jesus.

Holy Mary, Mother of God,
     pray for us sinners, now and
     at the hour of our death. Amen.

When Jesus was a boy, he lived in Nazareth with the Blessed Virgin Mary and Saint Joseph.

Jesus always obeyed his Mother and Saint Joseph. He always did what they wanted.

He helped his mother and Saint Joseph. He helped his neighbors too.

Jesus was very holy. He did everything only to please God, his Father. He wanted everyone to be happy.   It hurt him to see anyone poor, hungry, suffering. His heart was full of love for all.

Jesus showed us how to be good.   He taught us how to love and help our parents. He was always kind and loving to poor, weak, elderly and sick people.

I want to be like my Jesus. I will try to do good always. I will smile to make sad people happy.

Jesus loved everybody. He never hated anybody. I will love everybody, even those who do not like me. Many times I will say, "All for you, dear Jesus."

Jesus will help me to be like him. He will help me to be always kind and smiling to everyone.

With whom did Jesus live when he was a boy?   Did Jesus obey his Mother and Saint Joseph? How do you know Jesus was very holy? What was it that hurt Jesus? How can we be like Jesus?

Did the Child Jesus obey his Mother and Saint Joseph?
Yes, the Child Jesus always obeyed his Mother and Saint Joseph.

The Wedding Party

One day Jesus was invited to a wedding party. His Mother, the Blessed Virgin, was there too.

There were many people at the wedding. Soon the wine was all gone.

Our Blessed Mother was very sorry for the bride and groom. So she said to Jesus,

" They have no wine." Jesus felt sorry for them too.

Jesus told the waiters to fill some jars with water. Then he changed the water into wine.

The people at the party were surprised. They wondered how Jesus could make water into wine.

Jesus could do that because he is God.

At that time people thought Jesus was only a man. Only our Blessed Mother and Saint Joseph knew that Jesus was God.

Jesus now wished everybody to know that he was God. So he began to do wonderful things called miracles. This was his first miracle. By doing these wonderful works, Jesus showed his love and kindness towards all.

Why was our Blessed Mother sorry for the bride and groom at the wedding party? What did she do to help them? What did Jesus do to the water? Why were the people surprised? Why was it easy for Jesus to change water into wine? Did the people know that Jesus was God? What did Jesus do to make people know he is true God?

What did Jesus do to show that he is true God?
Jesus worked many miracles to show that he is true God.

Miracles of Jesus

Jesus worked many wonderful miracles. They show us that he is God. They show us his love for all.

Jesus met people who could not walk. He said to them, "Stand up and walk." And they did.

Jesus met people who were blind. He touched their eyes, and they could see.

Sick people came to him. He made them well again. He loved to help people who needed him.

One day Jesus met a funeral. A poor boy was dead. The boy's mother was crying.

Jesus was sorry for the mother. He went to the dead and touched him.

And the boy came back to life!

Another day a little girl died. Her parents loved her.

They were very sad when she died. The little girl's father asked Jesus to give him back his daughter.

So Jesus went to see the little girl. He said, " Little girl, arise".

And she came right back to life!

A man named Lazarus had been dead three days. He was buried in his grave.
Jesus said, "Lazarus, come out!" And the man walked out of his grave.

It was easy for Jesus to do all these wonderful things, because he is God. It is easy for God to work miracles. He helps us, too, when we ask him. God can do anything he wants to do.

Tell some of the miracles worked by Jesus. Can anyone work miracles? Why was Jesus sorry for the poor mother? What did he do to help her? What did Jesus do to make the little girl's parents happy? How did Jesus bring Lazarus back to life? Can any person raise the dead to life? How did Jesus make the blind people see? Why could Jesus make the dead live again? Why could Jesus easily work miracles? Do you believe that God can do anything?

39

Jesus was kind to everybody. He did very many wonderful things because he was sorry for people. He worked miracles because of his goodness.

One day many people followed Jesus. They had nothing to eat. Jesus was sorry for them.

So Jesus took five loaves of bread and two fishes. He told his friends to give the food to the people.

All the five thousand people who were there could eat. After all had eaten, twelve baskets of food were left over.

Only God can work such a miracle as this. We cannot do it. But Jesus did it easily, for he is God. God can do anything.

Jesus was kind to everybody. But he loved children best of all.

One day Jesus was resting. He was very tired. He had been doing good all day.

Some children wanted to see Jesus. They tried to go near him.

His friends said, "Go away. Jesus is tired. Go away."
Jesus saw the children and heard what his friends said.
Jesus said, "No, do not send the little ones away. Let
them come to me. I love them."
Jesus called the children. He said, "Come, my
children, come!"
Jesus loves me because I am a child. I will be a good
child for Jesus. He calls me. "Come!" he says.

Why did Jesus work the miracle of the loaves and
fishes? Why was it easy for him to work that miracle?
What people did Jesus love best of all? Tell the story
of Jesus and the children.

Jesus went about doing good. One day many people were around him. There were children also. So Jesus went to the top of a hill and began to talk to them.

This was long ago. But his talk was for me also. Jesus said, "I want you all to go to heaven. Love God with your whole heart. Love him above all. Give up things that you like best. Show your love to God in this way."

Then Jesus said, "Forgive those who hurt you; and God will forgive you." If someone hits me, I will not hit back. I will forgive.

Jesus said, "Be kind and gentle always. God will love you." At play time, I will gladly play the games others like. When someone talks to me, I will always answer gently. I will also help a blind person, and anyone else I see who needs help.

Sometimes I quarrel with my friends. From now on I will not quarrel. I will remember the words of my Jesus, "Blessed are the peacemakers." These are the Beatitudes. "Beatitudes" means happiness.

After this, Jesus told the people they must love everybody, even those who do not like them. He gave them " The Golden Rule." It is: " Do to others whatever you would have them do to you." This means I must love others as I love myself. I must love ALL others, even if they are different from me in their religion, their country, their language, or the color of their skin.

Jesus said, "Your heavenly Father knows your needs. See how he cares for the birds of the air. He loves you much more. You are all his children!" I am the child of God. I will always follow the Golden Rule. Jesus will be pleased with me.

What is the Golden Rule?

20   The "Our Father"

Jesus went on talking to the people. He loved them with all his heart.

He said, "God wants all of you to go to heaven. You must be good. You must pray."

Some people said, "Lord, teach us how to pray."

And so Jesus taught them the "Our Father". It is called "The Lord's Prayer," because Our Lord Jesus Christ himself taught us.

Jesus said we should pray, "Our Father, who art in heaven, hallowed be thy name. Thy kingdom come. Thy will be done on earth as it is in heaven."

In the first words, we remember that God is really the good Father of us all. He loves to hear us call him Father. Heaven is his home, and ours, too.

"Hallowed be thy name" is like saying, "May you be loved and praised by all, dear God."

When we say, "Thy kingdom come," we mean to ask God, "Be our king here always."

We pray, "Thy will be done on earth as it is in
heaven." This is like saying, "May we do what you
want in the same way the angels and saints in heaven
do what you want, dear God."
This is the first part of the "Our Father."
The "Our Father" is the best prayer we can ever say.
God loves to hear me say it.
Jesus made it for me.

*Why is the "Our Father" the best of all
prayers?*

**The "Our   Father" is the best prayer we
can ever say. Our Lord himself taught us.
God loves to hear me say it. Jesus made it
for me.**

21 The Pharisee and the Tax Collector

Jesus taught the people how to pray. He told a story about two men who went up to the temple to pray.

One man was a Pharisee. The other man was a Tax Collector. The Pharisee was very proud of himself. He walked up to the center of the temple to pray. He prayed loudly so people could hear about his good deeds. He was not talking to God. He was only praising himself. He wanted others to think he was good.

The Tax Collector went quietly to one side. He bowed low and prayed to God, "O God be merciful to me a sinner." (Lk. 18:13). He was not thinking of the people, but only of how he had displeased God.

Jesus said we must pray like the Tax Collector. We must talk to God. He is our Father. We can tell him how much we love him and want to please him.

In the second part of the "Our Father," Jesus taught us how to ask God our heavenly Father for what we need. We say, ***"Give us this day our daily bread."***

By these words we ask God for all that we need. We ask for food. We ask for clothes. We ask help in our lessons. But most of all we ask for help so that we can go to heaven.

If we are humble like the Tax Collector, God will listen to our prayer. He will give us more than we ask for.

How did the Pharisee pray? Did he praise God or himself?   Was God pleased with his prayer? How did the Tax Collector pray? Did he remember that he was talking to God ? Should we pray like the Pharisee or like the Tax Collector? To whom do we talk to when we pray? What do we ask God for when we say, "Give us this day our daily bread"?

Jesus taught the people to be good to others. He said God will forgive those who forgive others.

Jesus told a story about a king's servant. He owed the king thousands of dollars.

The king asked the servant to pay him back the money. The servant could not. He asked to be forgiven.

Then the king felt sorry for him. He forgave him the debt. In this way the king showed his goodness.

Later, this same servant met a poor man who owed him a few hundred dollars. He begged to be freed of this debt. But the cruel servant put him into prison.

The king heard how bad his servant was. He was angry. He called his servant.

He said, "I forgave you, but you would not forgive." The king had shown kindness to his servant but the wicked servant was not merciful to the poor man. So the king had to punish his bad servant.

In the second part of the "Our Father," Jesus told us to pray, ***"And forgive us our trespasses as we forgive those who trespass against us."***

This is like saying, "And pardon us when we displease you, as we pardon other people who displease us." So we must really forgive others!
Trespasses are sins. In the "Our Father," we ask God to pardon us for displeasing him in any way.

What must we do first before God will forgive us? Tell the story of the bad servant. Why did the king forgive him at first? Why did the king punish him at last? What are trespasses? What do we ask God when we say, "And forgive us our trespasses as we forgive those who trespass against us"? Where do we find these words?

Once Jesus prayed for forty days and forty nights. All that time he did not eat. The devil came and tempted Jesus. He tried to make Jesus commit sin. But Jesus drove him away.

If we feel like being bad, that is a temptation. We must drive it away, as Jesus drove away the devil. It is not wrong to be tempted. Our Lord was tempted, but he did not do wrong.

Temptation is not a sin. If we do not give in to the temptation, we do not sin.

In the last part of the "Our Father" we say, ***"And lead us not into temptation, but deliver us from evil. Amen."*** In these words we ask God to help us. We ask him not to let us do wrong, but to keep us always good.

It we are tempted, we must quickly ask God's help to be good. We may say the "Our Father," the prayer taught by Jesus himself.

When did the devil try to tempt Jesus? What did Jesus do? Is it sin to be tempted? How do we feel when we have a temptation? What must we do then? What do we ask in the very last part of the "Our Father"?

Say the "Our Father."

Our Father, who art in heaven,
hallowed be thy name.
Thy kingdom come.
Thy will be done on earth as it is in heaven.

Give us this day our daily bread,
and forgive us our trespasses,
as we forgive those
who trespass against us,
and lead us not into temptation,
but deliver us from evil. Amen.

The Last Supper

Jesus had many friends. From them he chose twelve men. We call them apostles. Jesus taught them well. He showed them that he was God.

The apostles loved Jesus. They knew that he was God. They believed all that he said to them.

But some others hated Jesus. They hated Our Lord because of his goodness. The more good Jesus did, the more the bad people hated him.

At last they said, "Let us kill this man, Jesus. Let us put him to death."

Now Jesus knew what the bad people wanted to do. He knew because he was God. He called his apostles together the night before he died.

The night before he died, Jesus ate supper with his apostles. While they were eating Jesus took bread. He blessed it and broke it. Giving it to his apostles to eat, he said, "This is My body."

As soon as Jesus said, "This is my body," the bread was no longer bread. It had become the body of Jesus, Son of God. It is the food of our soul.

What Jesus held in his hand looked and tasted like bread, but it was not bread. It was himself.

Jesus then took a cup of wine. He blessed it, and giving to them to drink, said," This is My blood."

All at once the wine became the blood of Jesus Christ. It looked and tasted like wine, but it was no longer wine. It had become the blood of Jesus, Son of God. It was himself. That is the Holy Eucharist.

The Last Supper was the First Holy Sacrifice of the Mass. Jesus offered himself to his Father as a sacrifice for love of us. Holy Eucharist is the best offering to God. I will offer Holy Mass for love of Jesus.

The First Priest

At the Last Supper, which was the First Mass, Jesus changed bread and wine into his body and blood. This most precious gift we call the Holy Eucharist.

Jesus loves us very much. He wanted us to have him always. And this is why he told the apostles to do what he had done. He said to them, " Do this in memory of me." By these words Jesus told his apostles to change bread and wine into his body and blood. By these words Jesus made the apostles priests.

Jesus did so by saying to them at this First Mass: "Do this in memory of me." Priests obey this command of Jesus when they offer Holy Mass.

The apostles were the first priests and the first bishops of the Catholic Church. Saint Peter was one of the twelve apostles. Jesus made him head of all. Saint Peter was the leader. He was the chief teacher and ruler. He was the very first Pope of the Catholic Church.

Jesus made St. Peter the First Pope

What words did Jesus say when he took bread at the Last Supper? What happened to the Bread? What did he say over the wine? What happened to the wine? Why could he change bread and wine into his body and blood? What did Jesus tell the apostles to do after him? What words did he use? By what words did he make the apostles priests? Who were the first priests and bishops of the Church? Who was the first Pope? What was the First Mass?

What happened at the Last Supper when Jesus said: "This is my body...this is my blood" ?
When Jesus said, "This is my body," the bread was changed into his body; and when he said, "This is my blood," the wine was changed into his blood.

After the Last Supper, Jesus and his apostles went to a garden. There Jesus became very sad. He was thinking of the sins of all of us.

Jesus saw all the sins the people committed from the time of Adam and Eve. He saw all the bad things they would do till the end of the world. This terrible picture in his mind made Jesus very sad.

Jesus was so sad that blood came out all over his body. The blood could be seen on his clothes.

We call the sufferings of Jesus his passion. The sufferings of Jesus made up for the sins of all: men, women and children. They taught us to suffer for others.

The men who were jealous of Jesus seized him from the garden. They arrested him. They tied him to a post and beat him with big whips.

They spat on him and pressed down on his head a crown of thorns. They made fun of him. Laughing at him, they called him many bad names.

But Jesus was silent. He suffered all these things because he loved each one of us.

If I love Jesus, I will never displease him. I will keep
smiling even when I am hurt, or sick. Like Jesus, I
will forgive anyone who displeases me.

Why did God the Son become man?
God the Son became man to take away our
sins and to help everybody to reach heaven.

The enemies of Jesus made him carry a heavy cross. He had to carry it along the streets. He had to carry it up Mount Calvary.

Jesus became so weak that he fell down several times. But they beat him so cruelly until he stood up again.

On the way Jesus met his beloved Mother. How she must have suffered upon seeing her Son!

At last Jesus reach Mount Calvary. His enemies then nailed his hands and feet to the cross.

They lifted up the cross and let Jesus hang there. For three hours he suffered on the cross.

While dying, Jesus prayed to God. He said, "Father, forgive them, for they know not what they do."

We call the day of Our Lord's death "Good Friday." Jesus died so everyone could go to heaven.

Jesus died in obedience to make up to his Father for all the times that people have displeased him by disobeying the Father. Jesus is our Savior. He loves each and everyone of us.

What did the enemies of Jesus make Jesus carry? Where
did Jesus carry his cross? What did his enemies do to
Jesus when they reached Mount Calvary? How long did
Jesus hang on the cross?   Why did Jesus suffer and die
on the cross?

How did Jesus take away all our sins?
**Jesus took away all our sins by his sufferings
and death on the cross.**

Jesus died on Good Friday at three o'clock in the afternoon. His Blessed Mother was with him. Good friends helped her to take down the body of Jesus from the cross. They buried Jesus in a nearby tomb.
On the third day early in the morning there was a great earthquake. Jesus rose and came out of the grave. Two angels appeared. The guards ran away for fear.

We call this rising from the dead his resurrection. And the day that it took place we call Easter. It is our greatest feast.
Jesus stayed on earth for forty days after his resurrection. He appeared to his apostles. He talked with them.
Forty days after the resurrection, Jesus took his apostles and other friends to Mount Olivet. He told them from heaven he would send the Holy Spirit. He then blessed them and went up into heaven. We call this the Ascension of Our Lord.

The apostles returned to Jerusalem. After ten days the Holy Spirit came down on the apostles. We call this feast Pentecost Sunday.

When did Christ die? Where was he buried?
What happened on the third day? What is Easter? What
did Jesus promise his apostles before going to heaven?
What is the Ascension of Our Lord? What is
Pentecost?

When did Christ rise from the dead?
**Christ rose from the dead on Easter Sunday,
the third day after his death.**

When did Christ ascend to heaven?
**Christ ascended into heaven forty days after
his resurrection.**

The Catholic Church

At the Last Supper Jesus Christ made the apostles bishops and priests. They were the very first bishops and priests of the Catholic Church.

Saint Peter was their head. He was the first Pope of the Church. After his death his successors were elected. Our present Pope is the successor of Saint Peter now.

Our bishops came after the apostles. The Pope and the bishops rule the Catholic Church. With the help of our priests, they take care of our spiritual needs.

At the Last Supper Jesus gave his apostles the power to offer the Holy Eucharist and to forgive sins. Even now, our bishops and priests receive these powers. Under the Holy Father, they take care of the Church. They take care of our spiritual needs.

They have done this in order to help all to be good and to help each other to be good. Jesus came on earth to help everybody to go to heaven. The Catholic Church teaches everyone "the Way" that is Jesus.

The Church does everything for Jesus.
The Catholic Church is God's Church. Jesus started it to help all people to go to heaven. In heaven we shall be happy with God, our Father, Jesus and the Holy Spirit forever.

Who came after the apostles? Who came after Saint Peter? Who rules the Catholic Church? Who help the bishops to care for our spiritual needs? Why does the Catholic Church care for our spiritual needs? What does the Catholic Church do for everybody? For whom does the Church do everything? Which Church is God's Church?

How does Jesus help everyone to reach heaven?
Jesus helps everyone to reach heaven through the Catholic Church

Jesus left us many ways by which we can receive God's grace so we can go to heaven when we die.

God's grace is a gift or present from him, which helps us to be good. Grace is God's living presence in us. It makes the soul holy and pleasing to him. We cannot go to heaven without this gift of God's grace.

Jesus left us seven ways by which we can surely get this gift of God's grace. These ways that Jesus left are the sacraments. Christ himself instituted the seven sacraments.

Jesus left the seven sacraments to the Catholic Church. The bishops and priests of the Church give the sacraments to us. In this way the Church helps us to go to heaven.

Sacraments are outward signs instituted by Christ to give grace. We can see and hear when they are being given.

Jesus left us seven sacraments, seven ways of receiving God's grace, his intimate friendship. Every time we receive a sacrament, it is really Jesus who gives it to us.

What is a sacrament?
A sacrament is an outward sign, instituted by Christ to give grace.

What does grace do to the soul?
Grace makes the soul holy and pleasing to God by making the Father, Son, and the Holy Spirit present in us.

31   **Baptism**

When I was a baby, I received the sacrament of Baptism.

I had my parents and God parents with me. In her arms my mother held me. My parents and godparents stood near me.

The priest prayed over me. He asked God to send me his grace, to make me his child.   Then he took some water and poured it upon my head, saying: "I baptize you in the name of the Father, and of the Son, and of the Holy Spirit."

My parents and Godparents signed me with the Sign of the Cross.

In that way, I received the sacrament of Baptism. I became a child of God. I became a Christian.

Baptism is a wonderful sacrament. When I was born, I had the original sin that came from our first parents. I could not go to heaven having that sin.

But after Baptism, I was made clean. That original sin was taken away. If I live a good life I shall go to heaven when I die.

Baptism made me a child of God

Baptism washed away original sin from my soul, and made it rich in the grace of God. My soul became most holy and pleasing to God. Father, Son, and the Holy Spirit dwell in me. I became a member of the Catholic Church.

I have received one sacrament: Baptism. I am preparing to receive three other sacraments. Soon I will receive the sacrament of Penance. I will also receive the Holy Eucharist and then Confirmation

What did the sacrament of Baptism do for you?

Baptism washed away original sin from my soul and made it rich in the grace of God. It made me a Catholic.

When Jesus went up to heaven, the apostles were still a little afraid of those who killed Jesus . They were afraid of his enemies.

But one day, while the apostles were praying, the Holy Spirit came down on them. And do you know what happened?

The apostles became very brave. They became fearless witnesses of Christ, ready to profess, defend and die for God.

The apostles went out and began to teach about the things Jesus had taught. They were not afraid of anyone. They were not afraid of death. It was the Holy Spirit who had made them strong.

Our bishop will give me the sacrament of Confirmation. It will make me brave enough to do anything for my loving Father, even hard things.

My Confirmation will make me strong and courageous Christian. It will give me gifts and fruits of the Holy Spirit. It will make me a fearless witness of Jesus Christ.

Confirmation means "making strong." My Confirmation will give me the Holy Spirit. It will do to me what the Holy Spirit did to the apostles long ago. The apostles became very good and helped others to become good children of God and of his Church.

What happened to the apostles when the Holy Spirit came down on them? Who will give you the sacrament of Confirmation?

What will Confirmation do for you?
Confirmation will increase in me the grace of God by which I wish to become very good and help others to become good.

69

33   The Sacrament of Penance

Baptism takes away sin. But it does not take away the
weaknesses of human nature, inclination to sin. Sometimes
people commit sin after Baptism. What did Jesus do to unite
them to him again? He gave them the sacrament of Penance.
It is also called the sacrament of Reconciliation, of
Confession, of Forgiveness and of Conversion.

We receive the sacrament of Penance when we go to
confession. It is a very wonderful sacrament. It takes away
our sins and reunites us with God, and our brothers and
sisters.

In confession we tell the priest our sins, how we have
displeased our heavenly Father, Jesus and the Holy Spirit and
hurt other people. The priest takes the place of Jesus.

Jesus gave power to priests to forgive sins in the name of
God.

I want to go to confession. I must first find out how I have
made God sad and hurt others. I must think, pray and be
sorry for them.

I shall ask Jesus to help me to think, I say, "Dear Jesus, I
want to know all my sins."

I also ask my Blessed Mother Mary. I say, "My sweet
Mother, please help me to find out how I have hurt Jesus and
others. I want to go to confession."

Jesus, Blessed Mother and my Guardian Angel will help me.
I shall find out my sins. I shall know what to tell in
confession.

Finding out my sins

I shall see what wrong I did in church, at home, at school.
I shall see what wrong I did with my eyes, ears, mouth,
hands, and feet.

What sacrament did Jesus give us to take away sins after
Baptism? When do you receive the sacrament of Penance?
To whom do you tell your sins in confession? What does
the priest do to your sins in confession? Why can the
priest do this? Who will help you find out your sins?

What is the sacrament of Penance?

**The sacrament of penance is the sacrament by
which sins committed after Baptism are
forgiven.**

71

Adam and Eve disobeyed God. God was sad and had to send them out of Paradise. He had to close heaven to them.

Their sin in us is called original sin. But this is not the only kind. There is another kind, called actual sin.

Actual sin is any sin we ourselves commit.

Adam and Eve had children. One of the sons, was wicked. He killed his brother Abel.

That sin of Cain was an actual sin. Killing is a serious sin. God punished Cain for it.

God is holy. He hates sin. He punishes the sinner. No one can see God if he has sins.

Heaven is our home where our Blessed Mother, angels and saints see God face to face. It is our most holy and happy home. If we always please God, we too shall go there when we die.

God wants us to be his good children. If we disobey him, we make him sad. Sin is disobedience to God's laws. Sin is to choose to do hurtful things on purpose. God wants us to choose good and stay away from what is evil.

It is wrong to fight or say mean words.
It is a sin to disobey our parents.
It is a sin to steal. It is a sin to tell a lie.

C
H
I
L
D

O
F

G
O
D

All these hurt God, our loving Father. They make him sad. We must be good and keep our souls beautiful. Then we shall find heaven open to us when we die.

Mistakes and sin are not the same. You might break a glass by mistake. You sin when you choose to do something you know is wrong.

Why did God punish Adam and Eve? Can we go to heaven if we have a sin? What is sin? Name some sins.

Is original sin the only kind of sin?
No, there is another kind of sin called actual sin.
What is actual sin?
Actual sin is any sin which we ourselves commit.

73

Mortal and Venial Sins

Some sins are serious. They are called mortal sins. They make God very sad. They separate us from God. People who do very wicked things are no longer the beloved children of God. They please the devil instead.

At night a man breaks into a store. He steals all the money. He is a thief. He commits a mortal sin.

God wants us to offer the Holy Sacrifice of the Mass every Sunday. It is a sin to miss Mass on Sundays and holydays of obligation. I can be excused only if I have a very good reason, such as sickness. Sleepiness, laziness, sports, outings and picnics are not good reasons.

If someone dies with a mortal sin, he will go to hell and will never see our heavenly Father. Nobody can help him. He will have to suffer there forever.

Some sins are less serious. They are called venial sins. They make God a little sad. They weaken our friendship with God but do not take it away.
A child takes some candy against her mother's will. She commits a venial sin.

WITH NO SINS | WITH SMALL SINS | WITH BIG SINS

How many kinds of actual sin are there?
There are two kinds of actual sin: mortal sin and venial sin.

What is mortal sin?
Mortal sin is a serious sin. They separate us from our friendship with God.

What is venial sin?
Venial sin is less serious sin. It weakens our friendship with God but do not take it away.

75

Jesus suffered his passion and died on the cross to save us from sin. He wanted to take away everybody's sins, so that all could go to heaven when they die.

Jesus loved us so much that he died rather than see us shut away from heaven.

If we please Jesus, in all we do, heaven will be always open to us. Little children can make up to Jesus for the sins of bad people.

For love of us Jesus was born of the Blessed Virgin Mary in Bethlehem and became one of us. He suffered hunger and cold. A bad king tried to kill him out jealousy.

For the sins of the world, Jesus suffered agony in the Garden of Olives. He was beaten until he was covered with wounds.

Besides this, Jesus was crowned with sharp thorns that went deep into his sacred head. Then Jesus carried his heavy cross to Mount Calvary.

To save us all, Jesus was nailed by his hands and feet to the cross. He was pierced with a spear and the last drop of his blood flowed out.

Jesus suffered all this because he loved our heavenly Father and us. Sin must be a terrible thing to do all this to our good Jesus. Mortal sin separates us from God and robs us of eternal life and intimate friendship with him. I hate sin.

Why did Jesus suffer and die on the cross?   What were the sufferings that sin caused Jesus? What does mortal sin do to us? Must we hate sin?

What happens to those who die in mortal sin?
Those who die in mortal sin are punished forever in hell. They lose eternal life and intimate friendship with God forever.

77

God through our mother Church, commands us to offer the Holy Sacrifice of the Mass on Sundays and holy days. He wants us to pray in church.

I go to church to talk to God, my heavenly Father, Jesus and the Holy Spirit together with my parish family. I must be very good there, for it is God's house.

The child plays in church. He looks around. He laughs. He talks to others. He throws things. All these are small sins. They are venial sins.

It is morning. The child wakes up and get out of bed. He kneels down and prays his morning prayers. He thanks God for his sleep. He is a good child.

It is night . A child goes to sleep. She does not thank God for the day. She is impolite to God.

A child goes to eat. He sits down at once and eats and eats. Then he gets up and runs away. He does not thank God for his food. He is not grateful to God. He is impolite and ungrateful to his heavenly Father.

What does God want us to do on Sundays and Holy days? What does he want us to do in church? How do naughty children behave in church? When should we pray at home? When should we thank God?

The Child Jesus always obeyed his mother and Saint Joseph. God wants all his children to be obedient like the Child Jesus.

We must obey our parents. We must run errands for them. We must help them. We must be good to our brothers and sisters. A child's mother asks her to take care of the baby. She does not want to do it. She murmurs angrily. She is a disobedient child.

A child teases her little brother. She makes him cry. She is not a good child.

A child sees some money his mother has left on the table. He takes some of it. He commits a sin. To steal is a sin.

His mother comes. She asks who took the money. He says, "I did not take it." He tells a lie. A lie is a sin.

A mother calls the children to eat. They do not
mind her. They go on playing. These children are
not obedient. They make God sad.

What must we do when our parents ask us to do
something? Name some of the good things we
can do at home. Name some of the sins that a
disobedient child commits.

The Child at School

Our parents want us to go to school. If we are good, we shall be happy to go.
At school we must obey the teacher.

A child goes to school. He does not study. He keeps talking in class. He makes funny faces and teases the other children. He wastes everybody's time. He offends God.

The class is praying. A child does not pray. She keeps looking in her picture book. She does not ask God to help her study.

A child breaks the flower vase. The teacher asks, "Who did this?"

The child raises his hand and says, "Teacher, I broke it." He is a brave child. God sees him and is happy. God loves a child who tells the truth.

The child Jesus played, too. How did he play? Did he quarrel and cheat at his games. Did he say bad words? Of course not!

Jesus does not want his dear children to be bad at their play.

Whom must we obey at school? Tell some of the good things we can do at school. Tell some of the bad things we must not do.

If I want to please God, I must be good.

I must go to Holy Mass on Sundays and holy days. I must thank God as his loving child.

Each morning I must offer myself to Jesus. At night I must thank him for helping me to be good during the day. At meals I must ask God's blessing. I thank him for all his gifts.

I must always obey and help my parents. I must be nice to my brothers and sisters.

I must obey the teacher. I must study well.

I must not tell lies. I must not steal.

I must play like a good child. I must not fight, hurt anyone, or say bad words.

I must not cheat in my lessons or games.

I must not destroy what belongs to other people. I must help those who need help.

I must never do anything that I would be ashamed to let my parents know.

If I am faithful to all these wishes of God, my Father, my soul will always be beautiful.

If I am not faithful to these wishes of God, I shall have some sins. I must find them out. Then I must tell Jesus how sorry I am for them. If I am not sorry, confession will not take them away.

I shall never be afraid to tell on myself. I shall always try to be a good child of God. I shall do only what will make God happy. I love him.

What are some of the things we must do in order to be good? If we have some sins, what must we do before confession? Will your confession take away your sins if you are not sorry for them?

41

The Bad King

God wants everybody to confess all their mortal sins.

Serious sins make Jesus very, very sad. We know how our sins nailed him to the cross.

But nobody should be afraid to confess their sins. Jesus is disappointed when he sees someone do something wrong. But he is very happy when he hears them confess their sins.

I shall not be afraid to tell my faults, because only God and the priest will know. The priest would rather die than let anyone else know my sins.

Once there was a king. He wanted to know what sins the queen had confessed. He went to ask the priest.

But the priest said, "I shall not tell any sin."

The king was a bad man. He said to the priest, "I will give you money, houses, and everything, if you will tell me the sins the queen confessed."

But the priest said, "No, I shall not tell the sins that have been told to me."

The bad king was angry. He told his soldiers to put the priest in prison. And they did.

The priest died in the prison. He died rather than tell even one little sin he had heard in confession.

And this is how all priests are. Our own priest would rather be killed than tell any of our sins. He hears our sins only for God.

Why should anyone be sorry for mortal sins? Shall you be afraid to tell your faults to the priest? Who will know that you have done something wrong? Will the priest tell anyone what you tell him in confession? Tell the story of the bad king.

42

How to Be Sorry for Sin

I have thought of my sins. I know what sins I have to tell the priest in confession. I know how often I committed each one.

Now I must be sorry for them. I must make up my mind not to commit them again. My confession will not be good if I am not sorry.

I am sorry for my sins if I can truly say, "I wish I had never committed them. I wish I could take them back. I will not displease Jesus again."

So when I know all the wrong I have done, I will talk to Jesus. I say to him:

"Dear Jesus, you can see all my sins. They make you very sad. I am sorry that I hurt you.

"I feel so sorry that I have not been your good child.

"I will do anything to make up for these sins of mine. I will gladly make little sacrifices to prove my love for you.

"I will be very good to my friends, and give good examples. You died for love of us, my good Jesus."

"O Jesus, forgive my sins! I will never sin again. I will always be your loving child. I want you to be happy. Help me to be good!"

What must you do to receive the sacrament of Penance?

To receive the sacrament of Penance I must:

1. **Find out my sins with the help of God**
2. **Be sorry for my sins.**
3. **Make up my mind not to sin again.**
4. **Tell my sins to the priest.**
5. **Do the penance the priest gives me.**

Now I am ready to go to confession. I do not worry even if I cannot remember everything. Jesus does not mind if I really forget. He knows how easy it is to forget.

I tell my sins. Most of our sins can be told easily, like this, "I was disobedient a few times."

But first I say an act of contrition. This is a prayer telling God I am sorry I have hurt him.

I say, "O my God, I am sorry for all my sins, because they displease you, who are all good and deserving of all my love. With your help, I will sin no more." This is an act of contrition.

Now I tell my sins to the priest.

If I have done something that I do not know how to tell, I say, "Father, I have a sin, but I do not know how to say it." The priest will help me.

When I have told all my sins, I say, "I am sorry for all my sins even those I have forgotten."

What is confession?

Confession is telling our sins to a priest to obtain forgiveness and to be reconciled with my God and with others.

After I have told all my sins, the priest tells me how to be a better child. I listen very carefully.

Then he tells me to do an act of goodness or to say some prayers. This is what is called my penance. This is a way of making up for what I had done wrong.

Last of all, the priest tells me to say the Act of Contrition. Then he makes the Sign of the Cross over me. This is called absolution. This means God is forgiving all my sins and making my soul all beautiful again.

As the priest makes the Sign of the Cross over me, I also make the Sign of the Cross. After this, I feel close to Jesus again. I have no more sins.

Then I go back to my seat. I kneel down and say my penance.

Then I thank God for my good confession. I say, "I thank you, my loving Jesus. You have forgiven me my sins. My little heart is all yours. Please help me so that I may always be your good child and never hurt you and my brothers and sisters again."

I thank also my dear Mother Mary and my Guardian Angel for helping me to make a good confession.

How do you make your confession?

I make my confession in this way:

1. I go to the priest, kneel, stand or take a seat by his side.
2. I make the Sign of the Cross and say: "Bless me, Father, for I have sinned."
3. I say: "This is my first confession" (or, "it has been two weeks or one month, since my last confession").
4. I confess my sins.
5. I listen to what the priest tells me.
6. I say the act of contrition loud enough for the priest to hear me.

What do you do after your confession?

After my confession, I say the prayers the priest told me to say, and thank God for forgiving me my sins.

The Good Shepherd

Jesus loved us very much. No one can love us more than Jesus did. Jesus suffered because he loved us. He died because he loved us.

Jesus told a story to show how much he loved us. The story is about a good shepherd. Jesus said, "I am the Good Shepherd."

At that time the shepherds stayed with their sheep night and day. There were many wild animals. They wanted to hurt the sheep. They always tried to catch the sheep and kill them.

A good shepherd would save his sheep from the wild animals. Even if he himself got killed, he would try to help his sheep. Jesus is the Good Shepherd. We are the sheep. The wild animals are the devils, who try to make us do wrong.

Jesus said a sheep might get lost. The good shepherd would go and look for his lost sheep. He would never rest till he had found it.

The good shepherd would go to save it, even if he himself got hurt. He would be very, very happy at having found his lost sheep.

Jesus is the Good Shepherd. The lost sheep is the
sinner. After confession, I feel like that lost sheep,
safe again in the arms of my Shepherd-my Jesus.

*Who is the Good Shepherd? Who is the
lost sheep?*

What do you feel after a good confession?
**After a good confession, I feel like the lost
sheep, safe again in the arms of my
Shepherd, my Jesus.**

After confession I remember that soon I shall receive Holy Communion.

At the Last Supper Jesus gave his apostles their first Holy Communion. They were the very first people on earth to receive Holy Communion.

Holy Communion is the receiving of the body, and blood of Jesus. It is the receiving of Jesus Christ in the sacrament of the Holy Eucharist.

In the Holy Eucharist I receive the body and blood of Our Lord Jesus Christ.

Our hearts must be clean, to receive God. This is why we go to confession as prescribed by the Church.

One hour before I receive Communion I must not take any food or drink. I may drink water any time I wish.

As I enter the church, I bless myself with the holy water, by making the Sign of the Cross. I go in quietly. Before going to my seat, I give due respect to Jesus in the tabernacle. This is to say " how do you do" to Jesus as I enter his house.

What is the sacrament of the Holy Eucharist?
The Holy Eucharist is the sacrament of the body and blood of Our Lord Jesus Christ.

What must one do to receive Holy Communion?
To receive Holy Communion one must:
    1. Have one's soul free from mortal sin.
    2. Keep the Eucharistic fast

The Mass is the best way to worship God.

The day of my first Holy Communion is the first time I offer a
complete Mass. This means that I give myself to Jesus. He
comes to me in Holy Communion.

1. At the beginning of the Mass the priest and the other
   ministers walk to the altar. Together with the people I stand
   and sing a song.

2. I make the Sign of the Cross. The priest welcomes the
   congregation with these words: "The Lord be with you."

3. I remember my sins. I ask God and other people to forgive
   me. I then sing or say the Gloria together with others. It is
   a prayer of praise and thanks.

The Liturgy of the Word

4. I listen to the Word of God in readings from the Bible.

5. I pay attention and listen to the priest's talk called the
   homily. It helps me to understand the Bible readings.

6. I stand and join the others to pray the Creed . I say what I
   believe as a Catholic.

In the prayer of the Faithful, together with others I ask God to
help all of the People of God.

The Liturgy of the Eucharist

7. We bring gifts of bread and wine to the altar. I add my own acts of love and sacrifices as my personal gifts to offer to God. I also offer my dear ones and everyone in the whole world. Thus we prepare ourselves to share a special meal with Jesus, who always loves us.

8. The priest offers our gifts of bread and wine to God. I thank and praise God for all of his blessings. I especially thank God for the gift of Jesus.

9. The priest prays as Jesus did at the Last Supper. Through the Holy Spirit bread and wine become the Body and Blood of Jesus Christ.

10. We pray the Lord's prayer together. This is the prayer that Jesus taught us to say.

11. We offer one another a Sign of Peace. This sign reminds me to live as Jesus teaches me to live.

12. I receive the Body and Blood of Christ at Communion. I give thanks and praise for the gift of Jesus Christ in the Eucharist.

I am going to receive Jesus Christ, the Son o f God.

He is the same Jesus who changed the water into wine at the wedding party. Now he has changed bread and wine into his body and blood.

He is the same Jesus who cured the sick, who fed the hungry, who made the lame walk and the blind see. He is the same Jesus who raised the dead.

This is the very same Jesus who loved the children long ago. He said to them, "Come!"
Now he says to me, "My child, come to me!"

I love Jesus I say to Jesus, "Come, my Jesus, come to me!"

I receive Jesus into my heart.   I go back quietly to my seat.

Now, Jesus is in my heart.   I speak to him with all the love of my little heart. I say to him:
"Dear Jesus, how good of you to come to me! I love you. I thank you for all you have given me. I thank you for giving yourself to me."

"I give you my whole self in return. I give you my mind, my body, my heart, and my soul. Teach me, so that I may never be parted from you."

"Please help me, so that I may always be your good child."
"Bless me, dear Jesus, that I may learn to love you more."
"Bless my father and mother, my brothers and sisters, and friends."

"Bless everybody, dear Jesus. Teach me to love everyone. All are dear to you."

"Stay always in my heart, my sweet Jesus, because I love you! Amen."

Prayers to Remember

The Sign of the Cross

✚ In the name of the Father, and of the Son, and
of the Holy Spirit.   Amen.

The Lord's Prayer

Our Father, who art in heaven.

Hallowed be thy name;
Thy kingdom come;
Thy will be done on earth as it is in heaven.
Give us this day our daily bread;
And forgive us our trespasses as we forgive
those who trespass against us;
And lead us not into temptation,
But deliver us from evil. Amen.

The Hail Mary

Hail Mary, full of grace, the Lord is with thee.
Blessed are thou among women,
and blessed is the fruit of thy womb, Jesus.
Holy Mary, Mother of God,
pray for us sinners, now and
at the hour of our death. Amen.

Glory Be to the Father

Glory be to the Father, and to the Son, and to the Holy Spirit.
As it was in the beginning, is now and ever shall be, world without end. Amen.

Prayer to the Guardian Angel

Angel of God, my Guardian dear,
To whom God's love entrusts me here,
Ever this day (or night) be at my side.
To light and guard, to rule and guide. Amen.

Morning Offering

O my God, my most loving and tender Father, I adore you. I praise you and I thank you for all your gifts. Please bless my every thought, word and deed and keep me good today. Amen.

Grace before Meals

Bless us, O Lord, and these your gifts which we are about to receive from your bounty, through Christ Our Lord. Amen.

Grace after Meals

We give you thanks for all your gifts, almighty God, living and reigning now and forever. Amen.

An Act of Faith

O my God, I believe all the truths which the Holy Catholic Church teaches, because you have made them known.

An Act of Hope

O my God, because you are all-powerful, merciful and faithful to your promises, I hope to be happy with you in heaven.

An Act of Love

O my God, because you are all-good, I love you with my whole heart and soul.

Act of Contrition

My God, I am sorry for my sins with all my heart.
In choosing to do wrong and failing to do good,
I have sinned against you.
whom I should love above all things.
I firmly intend, with your help,
to do penance, to sin no more,
and to avoid whatever leads me to sin.
Our Savior Jesus Christ
suffered and died for us.
In his name, my God, have mercy. Amen.

Ejaculations

Most Sacred Heart of Jesus, have mercy on us!
Come, Holy Spirit, fill the hearts of your children with your gifts and fruits.
Mother of Mercy, pray for us.
Jesus, Mary, and Joseph, bless us now and at the hour of our death.

The Apostles' Creed

I believe in God, the Father almighty
   creator of heaven and earth.

I believe in Jesus Christ, his only Son, our Lord.
   He was conceived by the power of the Holy Spirit
   and born of the Virgin Mary.

He suffered under Pontius Pilate,
   was crucified, died, and was buried
He descended to the dead.
On the third day he rose again.
He ascended into heaven,
   and is seated at the right hand of the Father.
He will come again to judge the living and the dead.

I believe in the Holy Spirit,
   the holy catholic Church,
   the communion of saints,
   the forgiveness of sins,
   the resurrection of the body,
   and the life everlasting. Amen.

The Angelus

V. The angel spoke God's message to Mary,
R. and she conceived of the Holy Spirit
  Hail Mary.....
V. "I am the lowly servant of the Lord:
R. let it be done to me according to your word"
  Hail Mary.....
V. And the Word became flesh
R. and lived among us.
  Hail Mary.....
V. Pray for us, holy Mother of God,
R. that we may become worthy of the promises of Christ.
  Hail Mary.....
Let us pray
Lord, fill our hearts with your grace: once, through the message of an angel you revealed to us the incarnation of your Son; now, through his suffering and death lead us to the glory of his resurrection. We ask this through Christ our Lord.
R. Amen.

Queen of Heaven – Regina Coeli

Queen of heaven, rejoice! Alleluia.
For he whom you did merit to bear, Alleluia.
He has risen, as he said, Alleluia.
Pray for us to God, Alleluia.
  V. Rejoice and be glad, O Virgin Mary, Alleluia.
R. For the Lord has risen indeed. Alleluia
Let us pray
O God, who gave joy to the world, through the resurrection of your Son our Lord Jesus Christ, grant that through his Mother, the Virgin Mary, we may obtain the joys of everlasting life. Through the same Christ Our Lord. Amen.

Hail, Holy Queen

Hail, Holy Queen, Mother of Mercy, our life, our sweetness, and our hope! To you do we cry, poor banished children of Eve; to you do we send up our sighs, mourning and weeping in this vale of tears. Turn, then, most gracious advocate, your eyes of mercy towards us; and after this our exile, show unto us the blessed fruit of your womb, Jesus. O clement, O loving, O sweet Virgin Mary! Amen.

The Memorare

Remember, O most gracious Virgin Mary, that never was it known that anyone who fled to your protection, implored your help, or sought your intercession, was left unaided. Inspired by this confidence, I fly to you, O Virgin of virgins, my Mother. To you I come; before you I stand sinful and sorrowful. O Mother of the Word Incarnate! Despise not my petitions, but in your mercy hear and answer me. Amen.

The Mysteries of the Rosary

The Joyful Mysteries
1. The Annunciation
2. The Visitation
3. The Birth of Jesus
4. The Presentation of Jesus in the Temple
5. The Finding of Jesus in the Temple

The Luminous Mysteries
1. The Baptism of Jesus
2. The Wedding at Cana
3. The Proclamation of the Kingdom of God
4. The Transfiguration
5. The Institution of the Eucharist

The Sorrowful Mysteries
1. The Agony in the Garden
2. The Scourging at the Pillar
3. The Crowning with Thorns
4. The Carrying of the Cross
5. The Crucifixion

The Glorious Mysteries
1. The Resurrection
2. The Ascension
3. The Coming of the Holy Spirit
4. The Assumption of Mary
5. The Crowning of Mary as the Queen of Heaven

Anima Christi

Soul of Christ, sanctify me;
Body of Christ, save me;
Blood of Christ, inebriate me;
Water from the side of Christ, wash me;
Passion of Christ, strengthen me;
O good Jesus, hear me;
Within your wounds hide me;
Separated from you, let me never be;
From the evil one protect me;
At the hour of my death, call me;
And close to you bid me;
That with your saints, I may be, praising you
Forever and ever. Amen.

Formulas of Catholic Doctrine

The Ten Commandments

1. I am the Lord, your God. You shall not have other gods besides me.
2. You shall not take the name of the Lord, your God, in vain.
3. Remember to keep holy the Sabbath day.
4. Honor your father and mother.
5. You shall not kill.
6. You shall not commit adultery.
7. You shall not steal.
8. You shall not bear false witness against your neighbor.
9. You shall not covet your neighbor's wife.
10. You shall not covet anything that belongs to your neighbor.

The Golden Rule

Do to others whatever you would have them do to you.
(Mt. 7:12)

The Beatitudes

Blessed are the poor in spirit, for
theirs is the kingdom of heaven.
Blessed are they who mourn, for
they will be comforted.
Blessed are the meek, for they will
inherit the land.

Blessed are they who hunger and
thirst for righteousness, for
they will be satisfied.
Blessed are the merciful, for
they will be shown mercy.
Blessed are the clean of heart, for
they will see God.
Blessed are the peacemakers, for they
will be called children of God.
Blessed are they who are persecuted
for the sake of righteousness,
for theirs is the kingdom of heaven.

The Three Theological Virtues

1. Faith
2. Hope
3. Charity

The Four Cardinal Virtues
1. Prudence
2. Justice
3. Fortitude
4. Temperance

The Seven Gifts of the Holy Spirit
1. Wisdom
2. Understanding
3. Counsel
4. Fortitude
5. Knowledge
6. Piety
7. Fear of the Lord

The Twelve Fruits of the Holy Spirit
1. Charity
2. Joy
3. Peace
4. Patience
5. Kindness
6. Goodness
7. Generosity
8. Gentleness
9. Faithfulness
10. Modesty
11. Self Control
12. Chastity

The Precepts of the Church

1. You shall attend Mass on Sundays and on holy days of obligation.
2. You shall confess yours sins at least once a year.
3. You shall receive the sacrament of the Eucharist at least during the Easter season.
4. You shall observe the days of fasting and abstinence established by the Church
5. You shall help to provide for the needs of the Church.

The Seven Corporal Works of Mercy

1. Feed the hungry.
2. Give drink to the thirsty.
3. Clothe the naked.
4. Shelter the homeless.
5. Visit the sick.
6. Visit the imprisoned.
7. Bury the dead.

The Seven Spiritual Works of Mercy

1. Counsel the doubtful.
2. Instruct the ignorant.
3. Admonish the sinners.
4. Comfort the afflicted.
5. Forgive offences.
6. Bear wrongs patiently.
7. Pray for the living and the dead.

The Seven Capital Sins
1. Pride
2. Covetousness
3. Lust
4. Anger
5. Gluttony
6. Envy
7. Sloth

The Four Last Things
1. Death
2. Judgment
3. Hell
4. Heaven

Prayers Before Holy Communion
Humility and Desire
You are God and Master
Lord of all the earth
Who am I, here waiting,
Poor and of no worth?

Yet you'll come and love me
As your dearest child,
Kneeling, I adore you,
Jesus, meek and mild!
Come to me, sweet Savior
Come to me and stay,
For I want you, Jesus,
Come, do not delay!

Faith and Sorrow

Jesus, you are coming,
Holy God, to me.
You, the One who made me,
Lord of sky and sea!

Too great seems the wonder,
Yet believe I do,
For your lips have said it,
And your word is true.

I am very sorry
I have caused you pain;
I will never, never
Hurt you, Lord, again!

Offering

Ah, what gift, I wonder,
Jesus, shall I bring?
I have nothing worthy
Of my God and King!
You are my Good Shepherd,
I, your little lamb,
Take me, o my Savior,
All I have and am.

Take my body wholly,
Mind and heart and soul,
Never, never let me
Fly your sweet control.

Prayers After Holy Communion
Thanksgiving and Adoration

I thank you, sweetest Jesus,
For gifts from heaven above,
But most of all I thank you
For you yourself, my love.

I thank you for your coming
So sweetly to my heart,
And beg you never let me
My Lord, from you depart.

And like a little angel
Within your heart I rest,
With eyes of love adoring
My gentlest, dearest Friend.

Trust and Offering

Put your arms around me,
Tired and weak I am;
You are my Good Shepherd,
I, your little lamb.

Let me lay my head here
Close against your heart,
I will be yours wholly,
Yours, my Jesus blest.

Take my heart and fill it
Full of love today,
That from you, O Jesus,
Never may I stray!

Love and Hope

Jesus, Lord, I love you
More than I can tell,
Not for love of heaven,
Nor from fear of hell;

Not for what you bring me,
Nor for what you give,
Just for you, all-holy,
Just for you I live!

Some day, Lord, I'll see you,
And in heav'n above
Join the angels praising
Giving love for love.

- Natividad M. Marquez

OUR MISSION HOUSE PUBLICATIONS
Books for the Catechists, Catholic Home and School
EXCELLENT IN QUALITY • LOW IN PRICE

MY JESUS AND I—BOOK — of 40 pictures in full color. A beautiful picture book to inspire young children **how to love Jesus as their best friend** and to teach prayers with the help of simple text and pictures on each page. The pictures and explanations offer many opportunities for discussion with your little child on so much more than just the prayers introduced.
Soft cover   5 x 8 inches - 48 pages.

MY JESUS AND I—FLIP CHART— The same 40 pictures in full colors. The heavy sheets are printed on both sides in full color and are bound very sturdily. 22 x 28 inches.

When I wake up

Jesus is near when I wake up
I make the Sign of the Cross
It is "Good Morning" to God

MY JESUS AND I—TEACHER'S GUIDE - To use with *MY JESUS AND I* flip chart and book. An outline of work to be taken up each week. Most helpful for busy, parents, catechists and teachers.

OUR CATHOLIC FAITH
An up-to-date Manual of Religion, excellent guide for religious educators, RCIA program, all those who like to deepen their understanding of Catholic Faith, an asset for your library. Adequately comprehensive - Written in an easy-to-read question and answer format. Size $7^{1/4}$ x $10^{1/2}$ inches - 524 pages text and illustrations in colors - hardbound.

ORDER FROM:
OUR MISSION HOUSE
Sisters of Mary Immaculate
118 Park Road
Leechburg, PA 15656
Ph.: 724-845-2828
E-mail:omhsmi@yahoo.com
www.omhsmi.org